Help Me Understand

What's Life Like in Foster Care?

Dwayne Hicks

PowerKiDS press™

NEW YORK

Published in 2019 by The Rosen Publishing Group, Inc.
29 East 21st Street, New York, NY 10010

First Edition

Editor: Elizabeth Krajnik
Book Design: Rachel Rising

Photo Credits: Cover, DNF Style/Shutterstock.com; p. 4 Tracy Whiteside/Shutterstock.com; p. 5 CREATISTA/Shutterstock.com; p. 7 VGstockstudio/Shutterstock.com; p. 9 Zurijeta/Shutterstock.com; p. 11 Oleg Golovnev/Shutterstock.com; p. 12 Blend Images/Shutterstock.com; p. 13 iStockphoto.com/ideabug; p. 14 Didecs/Shutterstock.com; pp. 15, 19 Africa Studio/Shutterstock.com; p. 17 LightField Studios/Shutterstock.com; p. 18 Voyagerix/Shutterstock.com; p. 20 Vitalinka/Shutterstock.com; p. 21 Spectral-Design/Shutterstock.com; p. 22 MAHATHIR MOHD YASIN/Shutterstock.com.

Library of Congress Cataloging-in-Publication Data

MAR 1 8 2019

Names: Hicks, Dwayne, author.
Title: What's life like in foster care? / Dwayne Hicks.
Description: New York : PowerKids Press, [2019] | Series: Help me understand | Includes index.
Identifiers: LCCN 2017050221| ISBN 9781508167143 (library bound) | ISBN 9781508167167 (pbk.) | ISBN 9781508167174 (6 pack)
Subjects: LCSH: Foster children–Juvenile literature. | Foster parents–Juvenile literature. | Foster home care–Juvenile literature.
Classification: LCC HQ759.7 .H53 2019 | DDC 306.874–dc23
LC record available at https://lccn.loc.gov/2017050221

Manufactured in the United States of America

CPSIA Compliance Information: Batch #CS18PK: For Further Information contact Rosen Publishing, New York, New York at 1-800-237-9932

Contents

What Is Foster Care? 4

When Is Foster Care Needed? 6

Foster Parents 8

Birth Parents 10

Brothers and Sisters 12

Family Rules............................... 14

Your Feelings Matter....................... 16

Talk About Your Feelings 18

Getting to Know You 20

After Foster Care.......................... 22

Glossary 23

Index 24

Websites.................................. 24

What Is Foster Care?

Foster care is a way to help children who have family problems. A child in foster care doesn't live with his or her **birth parents**. They live with a family that has **volunteered** to take care of a child in need.

Do you know anyone who has been in foster care? Maybe you, a brother, or a sister are in foster care. Moving from your home into foster care can be sad and scary. However, foster care can help mend family problems.

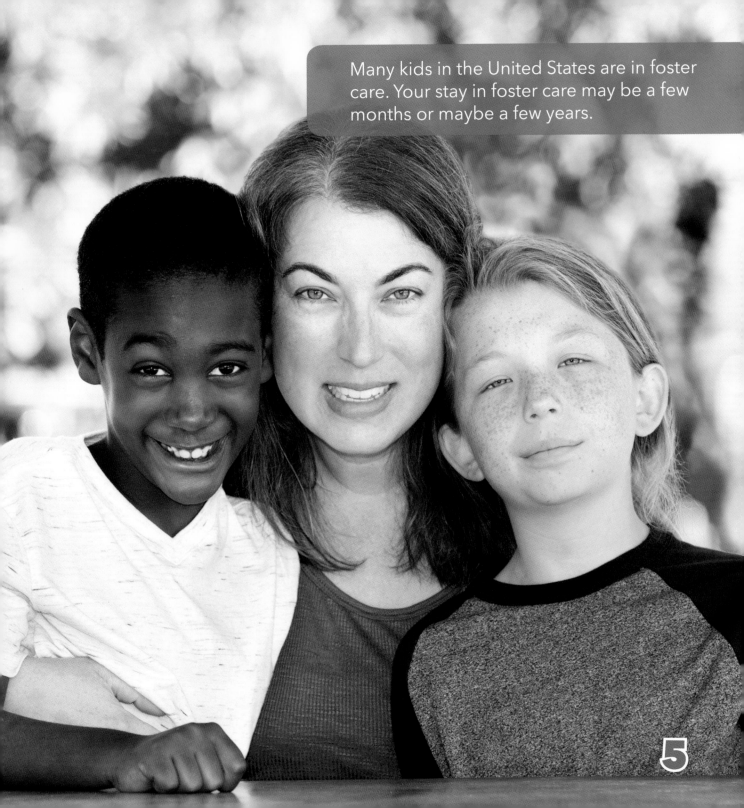

Many kids in the United States are in foster care. Your stay in foster care may be a few months or maybe a few years.

When Is Foster Care Needed?

Usually, grown-ups take care of children. But sometimes things don't work out that way. Some grown-ups are not trustworthy. These grown-ups may mistreat or **abuse** children. Other children are **abandoned**, as hard as that is to believe.

If an adult can't raise a child, a foster parent may be able to help. Foster parents will take care of the child until the birth parent can. Sometimes foster parents take care of children until they're old enough to take care of themselves.

Most parents argue, but some argue all the time. Some parents may even hit each other. Foster parents may need to care for children while parents get help for their problems. ⟶

Foster Parents

Foster parents are people who love to be parents! They often have kids of their own, but people without children can be foster parents, too.

Your foster parents will be different from your birth parents. They may eat foods you've never tried. They may not watch television or play video games. Give them a chance. You'll probably like them. Foster parents often choose the children they want to care for. They really want to help you!

A new home will mean new rules. You may be asked to try new foods or help around the house. ➛

Birth Parents

Foster care is supposed to be **temporary**. Many kids are put in foster care because their parents are going through bad times. When their parents are ready, the kids go back to them.

Sometimes kids can't go back to their parents. Sometimes parents have gone away or have died. Some parents are too sick to care for children. Always remember that it's never your fault that you're in foster care. And it's never your fault if you can't go back to live with your birth parents.

Foster care is tough for kids and parents alike. Grown-ups need to work hard to better themselves and get their kids back. ⟶

11

Brothers and Sisters

Foster parents often take in brothers and sisters to make sure they stay close. This doesn't always happen. Just because you don't live with your brothers and sisters doesn't mean you won't see each other. Foster parents make sure brothers and sisters see each other as often as possible.

A foster home may already have children living there. Maybe your foster parent has their own children. Maybe they care for other foster children. These children will be your foster brothers and sisters.

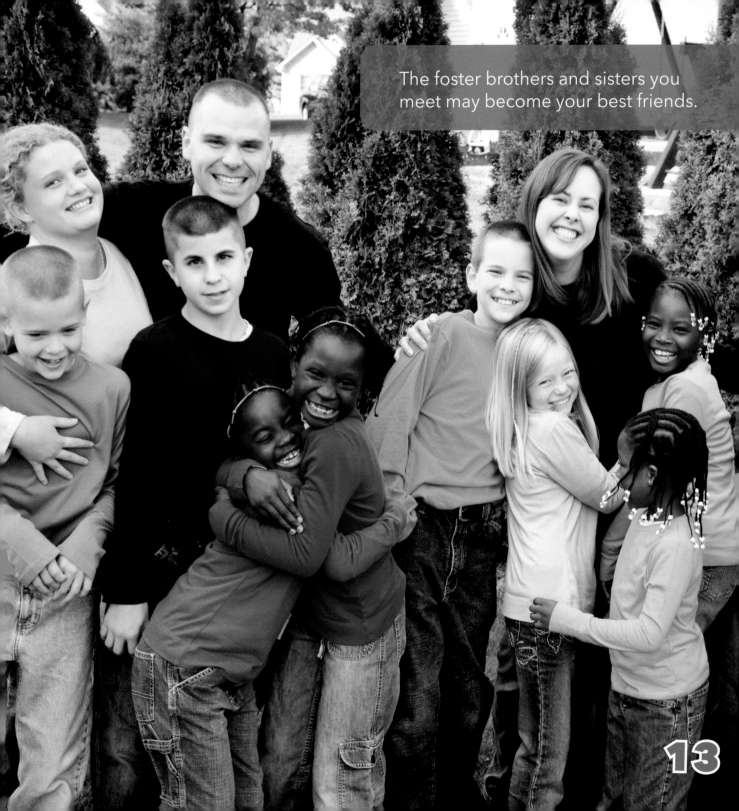

The foster brothers and sisters you meet may become your best friends.

13

Family Rules

All families need rules. In a foster family, people you hardly know can tell you to go to bed early and eat all your vegetables. You may not think this is fair.

You have to follow your foster parents' rules because you're a part of their family. If they tell you to clean the kitchen or do your homework, you should do as they say. Foster parents have rules because they care about you. They want you to be healthy and happy.

All parents, including foster parents, need to set up rules for kids to follow. Family rules help kids understand the importance of being responsible.

15

Your Feelings Matter

Foster children are sure to have a lot of feelings. You may feel sad and scared. You may also feel like you aren't loved or you may feel left out. If your new foster family has other children, you might feel different and like you don't belong there.

You might be mad at your birth parents. You might feel bad that you like your new family. Every foster child has these feelings. They are natural and normal.

Make sure you talk to your foster parents about your feelings. You will feel even worse if you don't talk to them. ⟶

Talk About Your Feelings

Whether you're sad, mad, or lonely, you should always talk to someone about your feelings. Talking is much better than shouting, hitting, or throwing things.

Try talking about your feelings with your foster parents, brothers, and sisters. If you don't feel comfortable doing that, you can talk to your caseworker. They help kids deal with their problems every day. They will help you find a way to feel better. You can also talk to teachers or a school counselor.

A caseworker is someone trained to find foster homes for kids in need. They are very concerned about your health and safety.

Getting to Know You

You probably don't want to be placed in a foster home, but it's important to be friendly and get to know your foster family. Remember, this family was ready to like you even before you arrived.

However, even foster parents can have problems. If your foster family doesn't take care of you or does something to hurt you, tell your caseworker right away. Your caseworker will find a better place for you to live.

You can get to know your foster family better by doing things with them.

21

After Foster Care

Each foster child has a different experience. Some stay in many different homes. They may not be happy in a particular home, or their first foster parents may not be able to care for them. Some kids remain in foster care until they become adults.

Some foster children return to their birth parents soon after being placed with foster parents. Other children may be **adopted** by their foster parents. Just remember that no matter where you live, you are a special, lovable, and wonderful person.

Glossary

abandon: To leave and never return to take care of someone or something.

abuse: To treat or use something in a wrong or unfair way; also, the act of doing so.

adopt: To legally become the parent of someone else's child.

birth parent: One of the two parents to whom you are born.

temporary: Lasting for a short amount of time.

volunteer: To do something to help because you want to do it.

Index

B

birth parents, 4, 6, 8, 10, 16, 22

brother, 4, 12, 13, 18

C

caseworker, 18, 19, 20

children, 4, 6, 8, 10, 12, 16, 22

counselor, 18

F

family, 4, 14, 15, 20, 21

feelings, 16, 18

foods, 8

foster parents, 6, 8, 12, 14, 15, 16, 18, 20, 22

friends, 13

G

grown-ups, 6, 10

H

home, 4, 8, 12, 20, 22

P

problems, 4, 6, 18

R

rules, 8, 14, 15

S

sister, 4, 12, 13, 18

T

teacher, 18

U

United States, 5

Websites

Due to the changing nature of Internet links, PowerKids Press has developed an online list of websites related to the subject of this book. This site is updated regularly. Please use this link to access the list: www.powerkidslinks.com/help/foster

24